Woodland Life to Spot

Illustrated by Stephanie Fizer Coleman

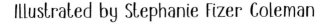

Designed by Lenka Hrehova and Jenny Brown
Words by Kate Nolan

The months given in the descriptions of some plants
and animals in this book show the time of year when
you're most likely to see them. They can be spotted
all year round if no months are mentioned.

If you find fungi (mushrooms), or trees and plants
with berries, remember not to touch
them - some are poisonous.

In the treetops

Wingspan can be more than a metre

Buzzard

This big bird perches in trees or soars in circles above them, searching for small animals to eat.

Jay

Watch for the patch of white feathers under its tail as it flies from tree to tree. In autumn, it buries acorns to eat in winter.

Tawny owl

Mainly comes out at night. You might hear the female owl calling 'tu-whit' and the male answering 'hoo-hc

Flies strongly, fast and straight

Noctule bat

You might see one just before sunset, although they usually come out at night to hunt insects. April–October.

Grey squirrel

Easy to spot scampering around woodlands, parks and gardens. Look out for its bushy grey tail.

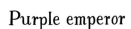

Purple emperor

This large, glossy purple butterfly spends most of its time gliding high up among the branches. June–August.

Forest floor

Lives underground in a burrow called a sett

Badger

Big and strong, with a black and-white striped face. It has powerful paws for digging – try and spot its pawprints in the mud.

Weasel

You might see this small, slender animal darting along the ground under the cover of plants and bushes.

White spots can wash off in the rain

Fly agaric

Look for its white stalk and spotted red cap. Grows under birch and pine trees. August–November.

Amethyst deceiver

This bright purple mushroom grows among fallen leaves. It gets paler with age or in dry weather. August–November.

Wood anemone

Its flowers have six or seven large petals, with pink streaks on the outsides. March–June.

leaves stay all year

Lesser periwinkle

Look out for the windmill-shaped, violet flowers, and long stems or 'runners' trailing along the ground. February–May.

Woodland edges

Rabbits live in big groups, in burrows called warrens

Rabbit

Watch for its fluffy white tail bobbing as it runs. It likes to nibble on grasses, young plants and tree bark.

Red fox

You might spot a fox in the early morning or late evening. Its bushy tail is known as a brush.

Turns brown in winter

Bracken

Look for big patches these feathery fe
leaf-like 'f'
the pla:

6

Elder

This tree's tiny, scented white flowers grow in sprays in spring, and become dark purple berries in late summer.

Sweet chestnut

In autumn, look for its spiny, bright green cases with two or three glossy chestnuts in each one.

Has yellow flowers in midsummer

Oval, toothed leaves grow in threes

Wild strawberry

Search low down near the ground for this small plant. Its white flowers become little red fruits. April–August.

Clearings

Young deer (fawns) have more spots

Fallow deer

These deer graze on acorns, grass, bark and berries. They're easily startled, so if you see one, stay still and quiet.

Makes a buzzing sound as it flies

Black and yellow longhorn beetle

You might spot this beetle feedi from flowers along woodland pa and edges. May–September.

Speckled wood

Flies in spirals as it chases other butterflies away, then comes to rest in sunny spots. March–October.

Foxglove

Watch for bees visiting its bell-shaped flowers, which have spotted patterns inside. June–September.

Never eat a foxglove – they're poisonous

Rowan

A small, slender tree with creamy flowers in spring and clusters of red berries that ripen in late summer.

Common dog-violet

Look for this plant's dark green, heart-shaped leaves. Butterflies like to visit its purple flowers. April–June.

Hedgerows

Bank vole

If you hear a rustling sound
under a bush, it might be this
little animal searching for food.
It eats nuts, berries and insects.

Short, round nose
and large ears

Hawthorn shieldbug

Search for this green-and-brown
bug on hawthorn trees. It eats th
leaves, and its young feed on the
red berries. April–October.

Red berries
in autumn

Honeysuckle

You might spot this climbing
plant twining through trees and
bushes. Its sweet-smelling flowers are
shaped like trumpets. May–August.

Primrose

Grows very close to the ground.
Look for its pale yellow flowers
and large leaves. December–May.

*ts of animals and
cts live around it

Hawthorn

This thorny tree is covered
in small, creamy flowers in
May. Dark red berries called
haws appear in late summer.

Common shrew

A tiny creature with
a long, pointed nose.
Snuffles through fallen
leaves, hunting bugs
ar¹

*Very small ears
and eyes*

Stumps and fallen trees

Velvet shank

In winter, these smooth, orange mushrooms grow in groups on dead oak, ash and beech trees. November–April.

Appears all year round

Turkeytail

Look for this fungus growing in layers on rotting wood.

Porcelain fungus

These delicate white mushrooms grow in groups on dead beech tree and stu~~s~~. August–November.

leaves have three heart-shaped parts

Wood sorrel

Grows in clumps on the forest floor, or on mossy logs. Look for its slender stems and dainty flowers. April–May.

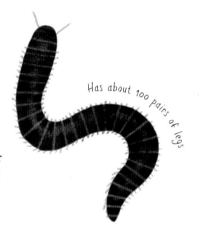

Has about 100 pairs of legs

Millipede

Likes to live in damp, dark places. If you lift up a stone or piece of wood, you might spot one scurrying away.

very large eyes and ears

Wood mouse

This golden-brown mouse eats berries, bugs and nuts. You might find the remains of its meal left on a stump or between tree roots.

Tree trunks

Chicken of the woods

This bright yellow, fan-shaped fungus grows in clusters on trees and stumps. June–November.

Holly blue

Watch for the silvery-blue flash of its wings as it flutters around holly and ivy plants. April–October.

Sometimes drinks at stream edges

Ivy

Look for this plant climbing up trees or walls in thick bushes. Its glossy leaves stay green all year round.

Short tail and black eyestripe

Nuthatch

You might spot one climbing up and down a tree searching for food, gripping the bark with its strong claws.

Great spotted woodpecker

Black and white feathers, with red patches. Listen for it in spring, when it drums on tree trunks with its beak.

Mottled brown feathers on its back for camouflage

Treecreeper

This little bird pecks insects from cracks in the bark with its curved beak as it 'creeps' up tree trunks.

Coniferous forests

These forests are mainly made up of conifers – trees that grow spiky needles and cones, such as pine trees.

Giant horntail

Female has a long 'tail' that's really a tube used for laying eggs on pine trees. May–August.

Looks like a wasp, but doesn't sting

Wood ant

Look out for mountain-shaped nests on the forest floor, built from leaves and pine needles. Up to 250,000 of these ants can live in each nest.

Pine beauty

Try and spot this moth resting among the buds of pine trees – the patterns on its wings help it blend in. February–May.

Scots pine

A very tall, straight tree with small, pointed cones. Its blue-green needles stay on the tree all year round.

Has tufts of fur on its ears

Red squirrel

This rare, shy squirrel is smaller than a grey squirrel. It loves to nibble the seeds from pine cones.

Has a creamy-yellow patch under its chin

Pine marten

An excellent climber that lives high up, in tree holes or old birds' nests. It mainly comes out at night. Very rare.

Broadleaf forests

These are mainly made up of trees that grow flat
leaves instead of needles, such as oak and beech trees.

English oak

In autumn, look for little
green acorns that grow in
cups and ripen to brown.

Merveille-du-jour

This moth's wing markings
match the bark of oak trees,
making it hard for enemies
to spot. September–October

Oak beauty

Look for the two thick brown
bands across this moth's wings.
Males have feathery feelers.
February–April.

Found near oak trees

Common beech

In autumn, its shiny, oval leaves turn copper-brown. Watch for squirrels and other animals collecting its pointed nuts.

Leaves often stay on through winter

Silver birch

Has papery white bark that peels in ribbons, and small, heart-shaped leaves. Long catkins grow in spring.

Sycamore

Leathery, dark green leaves. You might spot its winged fruits spiralling through the air in autumn.

Leaves may have dark red stalks

19

Mixed woodlands

Many woods contain lots of different kinds
of plants, trees and wildlife.

Holly

Look out for its red berries in
autumn and winter. Its thick,
glossy leaves have spiky edges,
and stay dark green all year round.

*Leaves are made up
of smaller leaflets*

Common ash

Its purplish flowers appear
in spring. You might spot
bunches of winged fruits
called keys in the autumn.

Common alder

Look for this tree near water
and in damp woodlands. Its
cone-like fruits stay on the
tree throughout winter.

Bluebell

Each sweet-smelling flower has six petals. You might see them carpeting shady woodlands in spring. April–May.

Hundreds of plants may grow together

Wild garlic

There's often a strong smell of garlic where these plants grow. Smooth, pointed leaves and star-shaped flowers. April–May.

Garden spider

Catches insects in a sticky, spiral web. Look for the cross of white spots on its back. June–November.

Spotting chart

Once you've spotted a plant or animal from this book, find its sticker a
the back, and stick it on this chart in the space below its name.

Amethyst deceiver	Badger	Bank vole	Black and yellow longhorn beetle	Bluebell
Bracken	Buzzard	Chicken of the woods	Common alder	Common ash
Common beech	Common dog-violet	Common shrew	Elder	English oak
Fallow deer	Fly agaric	Foxglove	Garden spider	Giant hornt
Great spotted woodpecker	Grey squirrel	Hawthorn	Hawthorn shieldbug	Holly

lly blue	Honeysuckle	Ivy	Jay	Lesser periwinkle
erveille u-jour	Millipede	Noctule bat	Nuthatch	Oak beauty
ne beauty	Pine marten	Porcelain fungus	Primrose	Purple emperor
bbit	Red fox	Red squirrel	Rowan	Scots pine
ver birch	Speckled wood	Sweet chestnut	Sycamore	Tawny owl
eecreeper	Turkeytail	Velvet shank	Weasel	Wild garlic
ld awberry	Wood anemone	Wood ant	Wood mouse	Wood sorrel

Index